The Little

GW01003483

ICT

Information and Communication Technology in the Foundation Stage

Written by
Andrew Trythall

Edited by Sally Featherstone

Photos and other illustrations by
Andrew Trythall, staff and children at
Sir Robert Hitchams School

Little Books with **BIG**ideas®

The Little Book of Information & Communication Technology

ISBN 1 905019 20 3

First published in the UK, April 2005

'Little Books' is a trade mark of Featherstone Education Ltd

Published in the United Kingdom by
Featherstone Education Ltd
44 - 46 High Street
Husbands Bosworth
Leicestershire
LE17 6LP

Printed in the UK on paper produced in the European Union from managed, sustainable forests

Contents

Introduction

Picture this **imaginary** situation from some years ago:

> A gleaming new computer has just been delivered to a corner of an early years setting. The children are excited, some go up and take a peek, some touch it gently to see what it will do. The children gaze longingly at the new toy that has arrived in the classroom, waiting every day for something to happen.
>
> The practitioners however are more wary; excited perhaps about what the computer can do, but conscious that no-one has come to set it up and show them how to use it.
>
> The computer sits there for a few days. One of the more confident adults switches it on, but the computer beeps at them, and flashes up some dangerous sounding warning messages. These messages glare out of the screen at anyone who walks past for the best part of the day, until the cleaner comes along, whips the computer plug out of its socket, and plugs in her vacuum cleaner.
>
> Over the next few days, the children begin to lose interest and wander back to the activities they know well.

Thankfully, this is **NOT** the picture in most Foundation Stage settings today, and many settings make very good use of the technology available to them, even when it is sometimes the oldest and most temperamental machinery available!

Unlike the children in the story, young children today are used to technology as a part of their everyday life. It is as normal and natural to them as reading a book or writing with a pen is to us. Technology to them is not strange, or frightening. They won't worry if it doesn't work, nor will they wait until someone shows them how to use something. They'll go ahead and try it out, play with it, and explore it, with or without instruction. Young children take technology for granted and they expect it to develop, and to do more new and amazing things every day.

Practitioners too are now much more comfortable and familiar with ICT. They use phones, microwaves, video recorders, e-mail, internet and cameras with confidence.

Practitioners also know that technology can do more for them and their children, but are sometimes unsure of what to get, or what to do with it when they've got it!

This is a little book of ICT, and we hope it will help you in the following ways:
- by giving you ideas;
- by suggesting activities;
- by extending ICT work across the Foundation curriculum;
- by raising confidence and reducing anxiety;
- by linking ICT to the activities you already do;
- by giving contacts for support, examples of work, free software;
- by suggesting hardware and software you could buy when finances allow;
- by offering simple ways of incorporating ICT in everyday activities.

The book will not tell you about how to use Word, or PowerPoint - it will point you in the right direction if you do want to learn to use them, but that is not its primary goal. This book is for anyone working with young children (at home, in pre-schools, reception clases and nurseries), for students of education at university or college, who wants to know more about how technology can be used to support children's learning. It is a book of ideas, all of them tried and tested with young children, and developed to engage and extend enquiring, creative minds.

This book is not just about computers! If it was, it would be very limiting, and would not encourage practitioners to encompass the wide range of technology available to them.

The author would like to acknowledge with thanks, the wonderful support of his Foundation ICT planning team, who have been meeting together for the last five years, generating and testing ideas. They are:
Lora Cann, Suzanne Odhams, Kate Mawson, Claire Holdaway, Jacqui Hardie and Sally Wilkinson.
Find out more about the author and his school on page 64.

The Little Book of ICT

ICT Health and Safety

It is important to bear in mind health and safety for both the children and yourself when using technology. Quite often we consider the children, but neglect health and safety for ourselves! Follow these simple health and safety guidelines for adults and children:

1. <u>Limit the length of time you or the children spend on the computer</u>.
   <u>Adults</u> should take a break after forty five minutes, children more frequently.

2. <u>Sit comfortably and change your position often</u>. Children don't have problems with this, but adults do! Make sure that seating and equipment are at comfortable levels to work at. Monitors are quite often perched on a specially raised shelf, and children are subsequently craning their necks upwards to see. This is uncomfortable, even for an interesting activity!

3. <u>Don't use just one finger for typing</u>.
   Encourage adults <u>and</u> children to use both hands, and more than one finger!

4. Check the cables:
   <u>Make sure electrical cables are tied well back</u>, can't be caught on anything and are left well alone;
   Make sure that <u>sockets are not overloaded</u> and that you have <u>clear access to the on/off switch at the mains so you can switch off power quickly in an emergency</u>. How many power sockets are hidden behind cupboards?

5. <u>Keep the work space clear of any clutter</u>; tricky but essential even in busy times!

6. <u>Make sure that light levels are appropriate</u> so you can see equipment clearly.

7. <u>Keep noise levels at an appropriate volume</u>. Headphones can be very useful to keep electronic noise down in the working environment, but <u>watch the volume levels on children's headphones</u>; they can sometimes be just too loud!

The Little Book of ICT

The Early Learning Goals for ICT

This could be the most misunderstood page in the whole book! In the early Learning Goals there are very specific references to ICT. These are:

Knowledge & Understanding:

- Show an interest in ICT;
- Know how to operate simple equipment;
- Complete a simple program on the computer and/or perform simple functions on ICT apparatus;
- Find out about and identify the uses of everyday technology and use information and communication technology and programmable toys to support their learning.

Communication Language & Literacy

- Know that information can be retrieved from books and computers.

Mathematical Development

- Instruct a programmable toy.

From this list, it may seem that ICT has a very small part in the Foundation curriculum. However, like the humble pencil, ICT is a tool that can and should be used **across the WHOLE Foundation curriculum**, and not just in a separate part. ICT is a wonderful creative tool, freeing up children and practitioners to interact together and learn about the world in new and stimulating ways. **Don't box up ICT into a computer corner.** Allow its many fingers to spread through the whole curriculum, opening up and offering all sorts of interesting and exciting possibilities for children and practitioners.

And remember, ICT is NOT JUST COMPUTERS.

Further Information

For **ideas on how ICT can progress** through different strands of the Foundation curriculum, have a look at the progression documents at:

http://www.hitchams.suffolk.sch.uk/foundation/progression

These web site pages give you ideas and activities in a progression for each of the Foundation Stepping Stones, and you will find the rest of the web site is brilliant for ICT inspiration!

The Primary Strategy CD - 'Learning and Teaching Using ICT Example Materials from Foundation Stage to Year 6' is a huge resource of **ideas, examples, documentation and video clips of children in action**. It is particularly helpful for the FoundationStage, and some of the examples are from Hitchams School; Tel:0845 60 222 60 or dfes@prolog.uk.com

1. A book about ..

A paper-based or electronic book about a class visit or event.

What you need

- writing software such as Word (for a paper based book) or Clicker 5 or PowerPoint for an electronic book

- a digital camera
- a scanner

Prickles had a bath.

Stepping Stones and Goals

CLL: use writing as a means of recording & communicating.

K&U: observe, find out about & identify features in the place they live & the natural world.

PSED: have a sense of belonging.

Additional Learning Intentions
Engage in shared, collaborative writing and reading.

What you do

1. On your next outing or walk, take a camera with you and take some photos of things of interest and things you find out about.

   Hint: Part of making a good book is taking a good picture. Try and take your photograph quite close up, and only include one or two children. Digital cameras are especially good at this, while still keeping the image in focus. Check carefully in the camera's view finder that you fill the screen with the subject you're actually photographing.

   Get permission from parents to use photos of their child in your class book. This agreement could be signed once to cover the whole year.

2. Each child could make one page, with the practitioner acting as scribe. Keep the sentences and text simple. Make sure the font and size of text is suitable for your children to read.

3. Word is probably the easiest program to try first. Use one or two digital images for each page, with a small caption for each picture.

4. The paper based book can be used in the book corner, on a display, or at an open evening for parents, as an example of the ICT and literacy work you do.

5. An electronic book can be displayed on a computer for children to read freely during the day.

6. Two programs that you could use to make an electronic book are:

   PowerPoint, which creates a series of slides

   Clicker 5 which has a special book making facility, and can automatically read out the text to the children.

There is additional help and advice for this activity on page 62

We sat on a bus.

More ideas

* If you're feeing ambitious, you could add speech bubbles to the photos. Word calls speech bubbles 'call-outs'.
* If you're creating an electronic book, buy a small microphone to record children reading the captions.
* Make sure your photo has impact. Crop off unwanted bits with the crop tool in Word or PowerPoint.

2. Turn into a clown

Use a simple paint program to help children turn their photos into clown faces

What you need

- digital or traditional camera
- a scanner
- a paint package such as Revelation Natural Art

Stepping Stones and Goals	Additional Learning Intentions
CD: understand that different media can be combined; choose particular colours to use for a purpose.	Begin to start manipulating photographs using ICT.

What you do

1. Take a photo of the face of each child in your group or class.

   Hints: The photos of faces need to be quite close up so they almost fill the screen. Leave a space at the top of the photo so that the child can draw in a clown hat. If you know how to rotate photographs, try taking photographs in portrait mode, with the camera on its side, to get rid of unwanted parts.

   Check each photo to see that it sits nicely on the screen when your child comes to paint on top of it. Many children's paint programs don't resize photos when you open them. To get round this, have your camera set to photograph images in as low a resolution as possible (normally 640 x 480 pixels). Alternatively, use an adult photo manipulation program such as Paint Shop Pro to resize it.

   Check which folder your paint program looks in when the child presses the 'OPEN' button. For example, Revelation Natural Art always looks in the My Paintings folder in My Documents. Copy the relevant pictures to the appropriate folder and rename each image with the child's name. That way children can find their own pictures easily.

2. Open the photograph of the child into the paint program; the child should start doing this themselves as soon as possible. Allow plenty of time for each child to experiment with turning themselves into a clown by painting on top of the photo.

   More Hints: Make sure the child understands the Undo button, if your paint program has one. This will allow them to start to self-evaluate something they've done, and to take it away if they don't like it.

   Keep a copy of the original photograph of the child elsewhere. This is particularly useful if you allow the child to do more than one clown photograph, a useful option as it allows the child to experiment more, and to have another attempt to improve their ideas.

   Encourage the child to save their work, and help them to type out their name in the save window. If they're doing more than one clown photo, show the children how they could use consecutive numbers after their name for each picture, e.g. 'Sophie1' and 'Sophie2'.

   Try Natural Art Software: Revelation Natural Art, uses realistic painting effects, such as watercolour or acrylic paints, and is useful for this sort of work.

   Graphics Tablets are a wonderful, relatively cheap way of painting more naturally on a computer, using a pen instead of the mouse. They're about £70, and one of the best is a Wacom Graphire 2.

There is additional help and advice for this activity on page 62

More ideas

* Painting over a photograph can be used in lots of topics. For a topic on jungle animals, try decorating elephants in traditional Indian style. At Easter or Christmas, try painting on a photograph of an egg or decorating a virtual Christmas tree; or celebrate Diwali by scanning in children's hands and painting on top of them in a Mendhi pattern.

3. 21st century role-play

Use ICT to support, develop and enhance role play in your setting

What you need	 the confidence to experiment and try something different!
🖱 electronic roleplay resources (see p13) 🖱 software that supports role play	

Stepping Stones and Goals

CD: engage in imaginative roleplay based on first hand experience; play alongside other children engaged in the same theme.

PSED: initiate interactions with others.

CLL: enjoy listening to & using spoken language, and readily turn to it in their play and learning.

K&U: know how to operate simple equipment.

Additional Learning Intentions

Increase awareness of ICT in their everyday surroundings.

What you do

ICT is everywhere. Children are exposed to technology all the time. Role-play needs to reflect this and to use technology accordingly.

1. Make use of electronic role-play toys. Many role-play toys currently on the market make good use of technology. There are electronic cash registers, telephones, microwaves, toasters, kettles, barbeques and more! These enhance the children's role-play dramatically, resulting in more enjoyable, more realistic, and noisier(!) roleplay.

2. Make use of old electronic equipment (e.g. mobile phones, cameras, old computer keyboards) or make mock-up machines of electronic equipment (e.g. bar code scanner).

3. Use your computer in your roleplay area. This might make you nervous, but have the confidence to try it out. If your computer is immovable, why not build your roleplay area around your computer. Here are a few ideas for using your computer:
   o make signs, labels and prices for shops
   o make a simple Word template using tables for an appointment diary, e.g. at a doctors
   o write menus in a café or lists of books in a library
   o order shopping 'on-line' using a drag and drop system
   o make placemats for cafes, or posters or other artwork to decorate and advertise
   o create background music for supermarket or café
   o type phone numbers, stocktake shop items

4. Use 'At the Vet's', 'At the Café', or 'At the Doctor's' CDROMs to promote roleplay. These are great CDROM games for initiating, exploring and generating role-play.

More ideas

* Record the role-play that's going on. Use digital cameras, video cameras, or tape recorders to record the activity. This will be useful for assessment, but it also provides a great opportunity to extend what the children have done, by using the recording in further work to develop language and numeracy, e.g. using photos of role-play for sequencing a story.

Further Information
More ideas and reviews of equipment:
        ww.hitchams.suffolk.sch.uk/foundation/roleplay
Example of a diary typed onto a computer by a young child:
        www.hitchams.suffolk.sch.uk/foundation/literacy/writing_examples.htm
Download example writing grids for doctor's surgery:
        www.hitchams.suffolk.sch.uk/foundation/literacy/reading_roleplay.htm

4. Become a DJ!

Use ICT to create, experiment with and talk about live music

What you need

🖱 music software or hardware that allows the user to compose in real time (i.e. live), such as:

🖱 a keyboard or Mixman DM2 (hardware), or

🖱 Music Brush 2 or music Box 2 (software)

🖱 2Play from Music Toolkit

Note: a lot of music software only allows children to compose in 'step-time' (see activity 14). This is where children set-up the composition in their own time, step by step, then press play, and **the computer performs it**. Real-time or live composition means the children have to perform it themselves (and therefore practice it beforehand).

Stepping Stones and Goals

CD: explore the different sounds of instruments;
recognise and explore how sounds can be changed.

PD: understand that equipment and tools have to be used safely;
show a clear & consistent preference for the left or right hand;
manipulate materials & objects by picking up, releasing, arranging, threading, & posting them.

Additional Learning Intentions

Practice & perform live music.

What you do

1. Children **practice and then perform a piece of music** based on a current theme in the classroom. Although it's important for children to have free time to play on musical instruments, they also need directed musical play which has purpose and stimulus.
2. **Stimulus for composition can be anything,** music for role-play (lift-off music for spaceship), music for reading stories (e.g. try getting children to compose music for each animal in 'Crocodile Beat' by Gail Jorgensen and Patricia Mullins), music for dancing Pixies (see activity 8).
3. **Try using these electronic musical instruments:**
    o a music keyboard – the Sing and Play keyboard from the Early Learning is very good, with a 'DJ scratch turntable' and drum pads.
    o Mixman DM 2 – a brilliant idea from Tag Learning. Electronic turntables that connect to a computer. Pads on the turntables can have different sounds assigned to them (including various world sounds such as India and Reggae). It's an easy way for children to create a brilliant composition.
    o Music Brush 2 – a music and art program that's **FREE**. It's a very simple way to draw and compose at the same time. The downside is that it only works on older Windows 98 machines, not on XP.
    o Music Box 2 – software from Topologika that has various music boxes for exploring music. The first box, called Sound Box, has a great, simple to use, seven layered, virtual keyboard, which can have a different sound (and they're great sounds!) assigned to each layer.

    o 2Play within the Music Toolkit - allows children to play a computer keyboard as if it was a musical keyboard, and to record and save their performance.

5. Write a story

Use story boxes as a stimulus for telling or writing stories using ICT.

What you need	
🖱 a storybox (see opposite for instructions and photos below) 🖱 a tape recorder which can record through a microphone	🖱 a digital camera 🖱 A word processor with a word bank, such as Clicker 5 or a concept keyboard

Stepping Stones and Goals

CD: introduce a storyline or narrative into their play; use their imagination in stories.

CLL: begin to break the flow of speech into words; show an understanding of the elements of stories, such as main character, sequence of events, and openings;

CLL: use writing as a means of recording and communicating.

Additional Learning Intentions

Understand that ICT can be used to communicate meaning.

What you do

1. **Storyboxes** can be based around a topic or in a stand alone scenario. Make them from shoe boxes wrapped in appropriate wrapping paper. Cut one or more sides down so when the lid is taken off, the shoebox opens to reveal a scene. Inside are characters and props to develop story telling. The characters could be Playmobil or Lego figures, peg dolls, plastic figures or small soft toys.

2. Use the Storybox scene, props and characters to develop a story.

3. Record the story digitally in a variety of media:
   o Use the tape recorder to record the children telling the story with the Storybox. Show the child how to operate the controls so that they are independent.

   o Use a digital camera to photograph different events in the story. The photographs could then be sequenced, or put into a word processor with captions or speech bubbles added (see activity 1), or made into a book.

   Note: Digital cameras score highly over traditional ones in many respects. One is that digital cameras have a macro mode. Macro mode allows the camera to take close up shots of small objects, such as a small Storybox, and still remain in focus. Macro mode is indicated on a digital camera by a flower symbol. Find how to use macro mode from your instruction manual. This function can have many other uses, capturing anything small e.g. minibeasts, children's construction models, or patterns.

   o Use a word processor to write a story. There are many young children's word processors available, but all of them have two important features: firstly, they have word banks that the children can use to build sentences, and secondly they can read to the child the list of words in the wordbank, or what the child has written.

   Note: Two common, but very different word processors with these feature are Clicker 5, which splits the screen in half and has the word processor in the top half, and wordbanks in the bottom half, and concept keyboards which, although a bit out of fashion now, are big pressure sensitive pads used with overlays (sheets of paper) with words on them. Clicker 5 is the cheaper option and works best with older Foundation Stage children; a concept keyboard works best with younger children as it is more physical to use, and can be shared with a practitioner.

Further Information
Find out more about storyboxes:
   www.hitchams.suffolk.sch.uk/foundation/literacy/storyboxes_&_taperecorders.htm
Find out more about Clicker 5:
   www.hitchams.suffolk.sch.uk/helps/clicker
Find out more about concept keyboards: www.hitchams.suffolk.sch.uk/foundation/words

6. What's it all about?

Use ICT to help children find things out and develop enquiring minds

What you need

- a large whiteboard, flip chart or piece of paper for questions
- information CDROMs, eg Dorling Kindersley's My First Dictionary, Become a Science Explorer, Become a Human Body Explorer or Become a World Explorer, or use the Internet
- 2Simple's Infant Video toolkit, which has 2Publish and 2Count

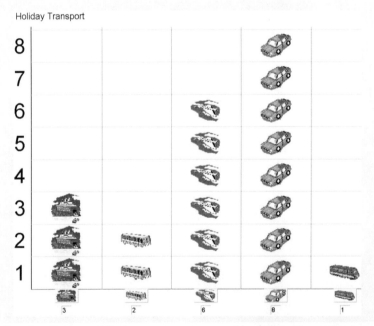

Holiday Transport

8					
7					
6					
5					
4					
3					
2					
1					
	3	2	6	8	1

Stepping Stones and Goals

CLL: ask simple questions, often in the form of 'where' or 'what'; know that information can be retrieved from books & computers.

K&U: examine objects & living things to find out more about them; ask questions about why things happen and how things work; comment & ask questions about where they live & the natural world.

Additional Learning Intentions

Develop a child's curiosity about the world around them, & examine different ways ICT can satisfy it.

What you do

1. As a whole group, think and talk about your current topic. This is particularly relevant when the topic has more of a scientific, geographical, or historical leaning.
2. Encourage the children to think and ask questions about the topic. This can be very difficult, especially if they are not used to asking questions. Encourage them to use question words, such as 'what' or 'where'. Model questions they might ask, or turn what they say into questions to support them.
3. Write all the questions they ask on the whiteboard or flip chart or on a big piece of paper. These could form part of a display later.
4. Talk with the children about how they could find the answers to their questions.
   This could involve:
   * observation
   * photographing
   * using books
   * asking someone
   * using ICT such as CDROMs
   * e-mailing an expert (eg a museum)
   * using an Internet search engine such as Google, Ask Jeeves or Yahooligans, a search engine specially designed for children.
5. Help them to use appropriate communication software, such as 2Publish to write and draw about it, or 2Count to do a graph, to display what they have found out.

Click here to start

More ideas

* Displays are not only useful for finished work, but also for showing children's thinking, research and ideas. Make an on-going display - add to it, and refer to it frequently throughout the topic.
* Print the questions out in large writing, along with pictures and writing the children have found on CDROMs and the Internet alongside the answers the children have made using 2Go or 2Count. This would make an excellent display, which can be referred to throughout the project.

Further Information
Useful search engines:
   www.google.com - also has useful image search
   www.yahooligans.com - children's search engine
   www.ask.com - a search engine where you can use questions rather than using key words
Infant Video Toolkit - available from www.2simple.com (cost £75)

7. Build a robot

Use Lego Tech Set and Remote Controlled Buggies to build a robot

What you need

- Lego Tech Set and Remote Controlled Buggies
- 'Harry and the Robots' by Ian Whybrow & Adrian Reynolds
- recycled materials to make robots
- space to make and move the robots
- safe space for storage of unfinished and completed robots

Stepping Stones and Goals

K&U: perform simple functions on ICT apparatus;
join construction pieces together to build and balance.

MD: instruct a programmable toy.

Additional Learning Intentions
Help a child understand that ICT equipment can be programmed for a specific purpose.

What you do

1. Read the story 'Harry and the Robots' with the children.
2. Talk about the way robots are designed and built for a specific purpose; in the case of the book they were built to blast Nan's cough.
3. If possible, show the children other pictures of robots, and talk with them about what they do. Look at the Robots of the World website, which has been written by children, for children.
4. Explain to the children that they can build their own junk robots, like Harry in the book. Get the children to think about what they want their robot to do, and build the robots accordingly. If you want some ideas, look at the Futuristic Farming website.
5. Now support the children as they buld a remote controlled robot from the Buggies and Tech sets. Show them how to attach the wheels and bricks to the buggies. Help them to explore the remote controls and the different channel numbers. Use the Lego Remote Controlled Buggies Website listed below to help you (and them).

> Note:
> The best way to learn how to use these kits is to take them home, and spend time playing to find out what they can do. Your family and friends will probably be very willing to help you!

Further Information

Robots of the World web: www.hitchams.suffolk.sch.uk/robots/world
Futuristic Farming web (examples of junk robot models):
www.hitchams.suffolk.sch.uk/schoolwork/futuristc.htm
Find out more about the Lego Remote Controlled Buggies from:
www.hitchams.suffolk.sch.uk/foundation/mybot/actionwheeler.htm
Three Remote Controlled Buggies and Tech Sets can be purchased from Commotion:
www.commotiongroup.co.uk (cost £120)

8. Dance to the music

Use ICT to inspire, support and develop dance and dancing

What you need	
Musical Leaps and Bounds CDROM	Pixies and Remote controlled buggies
data projector	dance Mats

Stepping Stones and Goals

CD: begin to move rhythmically.

PD: use movement to express feelings; move with control and coordination.

Additional Learning Intentions

Use ICT to inspire and develop a set of dance movements and to use ICT as a means of self-evaluating their own work.

What you do

1. Explain to the children that they are going to make different dance movements, and use them to describe feelings. Use your ICT resources to inspire different sorts of movement:
   o **Forward and back, side to side** – Use a dance mat to help the children create rhythmical movement with their feet.
   o Create various **'gestures'** (strong, still body postures) – use the dance sequence game in Musical Leaps and Bounds to help the children to develop ideas about some 'frozen' body shapes that could be used in a dance.
   o **Partnership work** – by programming the same sequence of movements into two Pixies, or by controlling two Remote Controlled Buggies from the same remote control, children can get an idea of how they could dance with a partner by copying each other, and doing the same thing.
2. In a cleared, large room, with a data projector and a laptop, use the Mood music of the TV game in Musical Leaps and Bounds to **play the children different styles of music**. The children respond using movements and gestures they have developed earlier, thinking carefully about the mood of piece, e.g. sad, happy.
3. Then **switch the television on in Musical Leaps and Bounds** to see how the dog is responding to that particular style of music.

More ideas

* Use a video or digital video camera to record the children's movements to the different styles of music. Play some of the video back and talk to the children about what was good, and how they could improve.

Further Information
Musical Leaps & Bounds from Granada Learning:
   www.granada-learning.com (cost £39)
Find out more about the Remote Controlled Buggy and the Tech Machines set:
   www.hitchams.suffolk.sch.uk/foundation/mybot/actionwheeler.htm
Three Remote Controlled Buggies and Tech Sets can be purchased from Commotion:
   www.commotiongroup.co.uk (cost £120)
Pixies available from www.swallow.co.uk (cost £136)

9. Shape and space

Use ICT to find out more about shapes and how they relate to each other

<table>
<tr><td colspan="2">

What you need

🖱 My World or My World 3 Tiles screen

🖱 Clicker 5; download mathematical shape grids from Clicker Grids for Learning

</td><td>

🖱 Drawing program, eg 2Paint or Revelation Natural Art

🖱 Pixies, sellotape, thick felts and sugar paper

🖱 2Go – part of the 2Simple Infant Video Toolkit

</td></tr>
</table>

Flowers
by Isabel

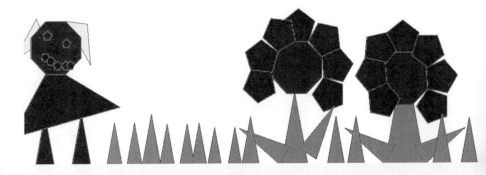

Stepping Stones and Goals

MD: use shapes appropriately for tasks; begin to talk about shapes of everyday objects;
use appropriate shape to make representational models or more elaborate shapes;
use language such as 'circle' or 'bigger' to describe the shape & size of solids & flat shapes.

CD: explore colour, texture, shape, form & space in 2 or 3 dimensions.

Additional Learning Intentions
Use ICT to help find out about shapes.

What you do

Here are some different ways to explore 2D shape with the children. You can do some or all of them, depending on the age of the children, your time and resources. They also fit together well into one session.

o Use the My World Tiles screen to build pictures out of shapes. The original My World Tiles screen is actually better, and more fun for the children, as is gives the children a wider range of shapes to explore (so many that you might want to limit it to only one set), and allows you to do more with them (flip, rotate and resize). The new My World 3 Tiles screen has fewer shapes, and only allows you to flip and rotate.

o Clicker 5 is a very good writing program that contains word banks to help the children make sentences. You can also download resources from the Internet. One of them, called 'Naming Shapes' can be used to generate simple sentences to describe simple shapes.

o Most drawing programs, such as Revelation Natural Art or 2Paint (part of the 2Simple Infant Video Toolkit), have tools for creating rectangular and circular shapes. Fill a page with unfilled, overlapping squares, circles, oblongs and ovals with different coloured frames. Then use the fill tool to fill the new shapes made from overlapping with different colours. You'll end up with a piece of art work a bit like a Mondrian!

Hint: If you're using 2Paint, use the options screen (Ctrl-Shift -o) to change from 'Classic Felt Tips' to 'Tools'. Then you will be able to draw rectangular and circular shapes.

o Use 2Simple's 2Go program to investigate different shapes. If you look at the 2Go website listed on P62, you can download a workcard to support the children in this, which starts quite easily, and builds upon the skills the children know as they work through it.

o Try sellotaping a pen to the back of the Pixie and getting the Pixie to draw shapes, such as circles (easy) and squares or rectangles (much harder). There are programmable Pixie cards that can be used to make squares and rectangles and video clip examples to watch on the Pixie Website listed on P62.

o Using the Pixie and the 2Go program at the same time in your group allows your children to make the transition from the concrete (in this case Pixies) to the abstract or virtual (2Go on the computer) more easily.

There is additional help and advice for this activity on page 62

This shape is called	a hexagon	It has	
	a rectangle	7 5 3 1	
	a triangle		
	a square	9 6 4 2	
	a circle	straight sides	.

10. Our world

Use ICT to help children explore, investigate and comment on the world we live in

What you need

Confidence - often when you start this project, you don't know where it's going to go! Be confident in this, & remember the pattern to follow:
* explore your locality
* identify a concern or need within the locality
* research the concern & compare with another locality
* enable the children to make a difference
* 2Publish from 2Simple's Infant Video Toolkit
* Pixies or Remote controlled buggies
* photographs of parts of the locality (shops, health centre etc.)
* e-mail or internet access
* digital camera

We wanta biger park

Stepping Stones and Goals

CLL: initiate a conversation, negotiate positions, pay attention to and take account of others views.

K&U: observe, find out about and identify features in the place they live; find out about their environment & talk about likes & dislikes.

PSED: talk freely about their home & community; show care & concern for others, living things & the environment.

Additional Learning Intentions
Empower children to change their local environment or community, using ICT.

What you do

1. Explore your local area.
   - Walk around your locality, observing, and discussing. Encourage children to identify their favourite and least favourite places. Take photographs of these places as you walk around.
   - Explore your locality 'virtually' back in your Foundation setting. Make a mini-locality using the photographs taken stuck to cereal packets, Pixies (see activity 9 for more information) or Remote Controlled buggies (see Activity 8 for more information) for cars, and toy people. Roleplay the favourite and least favourite places, and discuss what and why.
   - Ask a visitor in to talk about what they do in the locality. Get them to talk about things they like and dislike. Try and find someone who has lived in the area for a long time, and they can tell the children about how the locality has changed, and whether the changes are for the best or for the worst. If you have a video camera this can be recorded to remind the children.
   - Use the 2Publish screen that is split into two halves. Get the children to write/draw about something they like about their locality on one side, and something they dislike on the other (to get to the different 2Publish screens click the New Page button in the top left hand corner).

2. As a whole class, identify a common concern the children have. This could be to do with transport, noise or litter pollution, crime, wildlife, lack of places to play, and many more. They then could….
   - E-mail a Foundation setting in another part of the country (or another country!). Emailing activities always work best with a practitioner you know, and then you know they're going to be reliable. Use a data projector and write it together, telling the other school what people like and dislike about your locality. Finish the email with some relevant questions, finding out if they have the same problem, and what they did about it.
   - Try and quantify the problem, by graphing it. Use 2Count from 2Simple or something similar. This may be a graph of the different types of traffic that pass by, or how many and what people feel about an issue.
   - Have a visitor who knows more about what the children are concerned about. Again, this could be videoed for later use.
   - Use a drawing program to draw how they would like to change something, e.g. like designing a new place to play.

3. Try to empower the children to become actively involved in their community, and help them realise that they can make a difference, e.g. make a poster or car sticker, write a letter, have an assembly for parents, make a joint book with another setting, celebrate differences and similarities.

There is additional help and advice for this activity on page 63

11. Space exploration

Use a variety of ICT tools creatively to explore the planets and outer space

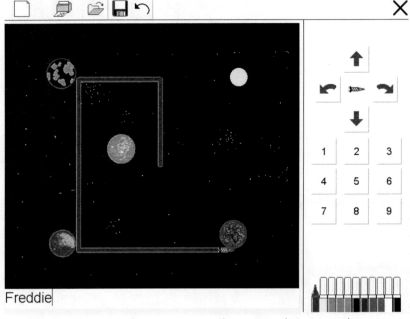

Freddie

Stepping Stones and Goals

PSED: have a strong exploratory impulse.

MD: observe & use positional language.

K&U: find out about, & identify, some features of living things, objects & events they observe.

CD: introduce a storyline or narrative into their play.

Additional Learning Intentions

Develop children's imagination and creativity through their natural curiosity about space.

What you do

1. Build a role-play spaceship from boxes or other construction materials indoors or outside. Role-play some different parts of a space adventure.
2. Talk about some good places to go, and find out about them by using the NASA Kids website, or suitable CDROM to investigate planets and moons they could visit
3. Build a space rocket on screen or a robot. Use My World Tiles screen, or Lego Mybots or Lego Remote Controlled Buggies to build a space rocket that the children would like to fly.
4. Plan your journey. Use 2Go from 2Simple, click the New Page button, and open the space rocket/planet game. Drive the space rocket around the planet. Remember that you have options for different types of controls to make this easier or harder (press 'Ctrl – Shift Key – letter o' buttons).
5. Go on a journey to a planet. Use roleplay equipment (electronic where possible) to travel to a planet. Electronic ideas could be:
   o completing a space travel logbook on the computer;
   o talking to 'Ground Control' through headphones and microphones, taking messages and passing them on to others on board;
   o using space sound effects on tape, CDROM, computer or keyboard;
   o using a calculator to calculate how fast they're going, and how far it is to get there.
6. When you get there make a planetary surface by using an overhead projector. Put a variety of transparent or opaque objects on the OHP and project a lunar landscape onto a wall. Create a new strange world. Project it big and the children can play and explore 'inside' the projection.
7. Make your journey home. Take pictures of your environment, and use them in StoryMaker from Spa software, to create stories about aliens landing when you get home. StoryMaker has lots of alien clipart, and speech bubbles, so children can make talking stories with a computerised voice.

There is additional help and advice for this activity on page 63

More ideas

* Take a photograph of the children in their space scene while using the overhead projector(turn the flash off on your digital camera). This photograph could be opened up in a drawing program on a computer, and painted over or have clipart added.

12. Now that's a thought!

Use ICT to explore stories and help children develop their thinking skills

What you need
You need time and patience. It takes a long time for children to develop good questioning skills, but keep at it, as the benefits extend right across the curriculum
- A range of stories, either on the Internet, CDROM or books, which convey meaning, thoughts or feelings
- whiteboard, or a large sheet of paper for questions and ideas
- children's brainstorming software, such as Kidspiration
- data projector (optional)

cover

1

Here are Mum and Dad Swan. They are looking for a place to make a nest. Why do they want to make a nest

next page

2

Stepping Stones and Goals
PSED: be confident to try new activities, initiate ideas and speak in a familiar group;
respond to significant experiences, showing a range of feelings when appropriate.
CLL: interact with others, negotiating plans and activities and taking turns in conversation;
listen with enjoyment, responding to what they have heard by comments, questions or actions;
use talk to organise, sequence & clarify thinking, ideas, feelings & events.

The Little Book of ICT

What you do

1. **Develop questioning techniques** using some of these ideas:
   - o Read a story to a group or whole class, such as 'The Swan Story' from the Nature Grid Web site. Use a data projector so that every child can see. If you have an Interactive Whiteboard, encourage the children to interact with the story.
   - o Get the children to start asking questions about the story. Teach the children the question words to help them. Model some questions to demonstrate the sorts of questions that they could ask. Don't answer the questions, collect them by writing them all down on a large sheet of paper.

   Hint: If you feel less confident, use the Nature Grid Website - many of the stories on this site come with examples of different types of questions.

2. **Extend the children's questions.** Move them on from the basic, 'Where did he go?' to 'Why did he go?'.

3. Try to **extend the questioning further** by exploring themes in the book, e.g. move the question from 'Why did Sebastian Swan feel sad?' to 'What makes you sad?'.

4. **Spend time talking about the answers** to these extended questions. Develop the confidence of children to participate, and help the children to understand that what they all say has value.

5. **Let the children plan some of your topic with you:**
   - o Use some child friendly brainstorming software, such as Kidspiration, on an interactive whiteboard so everyone can see it building up as you jot down things that children already know, and things they want to explore further. Use the brainstorm to inform your planning.
   - o At regular intervals throughout the topic, refer back to the brainstorm to see what's been covered, and where the children want to go next. Children could also add to the brainstorm things that they have found out, and new areas they want to explore. You could use an interactive whiteboard so everyone can see the topic building up.

Further Information

Kidspiration available from Tag Learning -
   www.taglearning.com (cost £59.95)
Good internet stories:
   Nature Grid: www.naturegrid.org.uk/infant/
   Little Animals Activity Centre: www.bbc.co.uk/schools/laac
CDROM stories:
   Just Grandma and Me, available from REM, www.r-e-m.co.uk (cost £20)
   Little Monster Goes to School, available from REM, www.r-e-m.co.uk (cost approx. £20)
   PB Bear, now deleted (unfortunately), but you might have an old copy in school somewhere (they're like gold dust!)

13. Colour matching

Use ICT to support and develop children's understanding of colour

Stepping Stones and Goals

K&U: examine objects & living things to find out more about them.

CD: explore what happens when they mix colours;
choose particular colours for a purpose.

MD: show awareness of symmetry.

Additional Learning Intentions
Use the natural colour, patterns and symmetry of flowers to inspire curiosity and creativity.

What you do

1. Use the Clicker 5 grid called 'Colours' (download it from Clicker Grids for Learning) to help children to recognise and match colours.

2. Do a survey of the different colours of flowers, e.g. how many different types of flowers are yellow etc.
   Impress upon the children that they must never pick wild flowers. Instead they can take close up photographs of them using the macro mode on a digital camera. See Activity 5 for more about Macro mode.

   Hint: Always encourage the children to use the digital camera to take their own photographs. This can be scary ("Argh! They might drop it!"). Use a camera strap so if they do drop it, it won't hit the ground! It is also a good idea to take a backup photo of the same thing after the child has taken it, as children sometimes miss the most important part.

3. Once back indoors, look at the photographs more closely. Print out the different types of flowers. Make a pictogram of the printouts to find out how many flowers are a particular colour.

4. Use 2Count to make a colour graph on the computer.

   Hint: It's a very valuable ICT process for the children to do something in real life, and then to do the same thing using ICT as it allows the children to compare the processes, and the advantages (and disadvantages!) of using ICT.

5. Look at the way some petals have stripes and spots on them. Demonstrate how they can make their own flower design. Open the macro photographs of flowers in a paint package, such as Revelation Natural Art and paint over the top of the flowers to add spots, stripes and patterns.

6. Revelation Natural Art has a great colour mixing facility which imitates the use of a mixing palette in art. Older children could look at Vincent van Gogh's sunflower pictures and then paint their own 'still life' flower pictures by mixing and matching the colours of a flower using Revelation Natural Art's colour mixing facility.

More ideas

* Introduce the idea of symmetry to the children, and how all the flowers they've seen are the same on both sides. Use a paint packages symmetry tool to paint symmetrical flowers.

There is additional help and advice for this activity on page 63

The Little Book of ICT

14. The next Mozart?

Help children to develop their musical talents using ICT

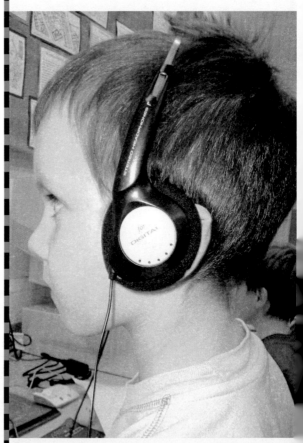

What you need

🖱 a piece of music which supports a current topic you are doing.
Possible ideas are:
* Saint-Saens - Carnival of the Animals for a Minibeasts/Jungles topic
* Vivaldi – Four Seasons for harvest, Autumn, Spring topics
* Electronic music (e.g. Jean Michelle Jarre) for anything mechanical, robots, transport etc.
* Prokofiev – Peter & the Wolf – Fairy Tales, traditional stories etc.

🖱 music composition software which allows children to compose in step time (where you add notes step-by-step)
Examples could be:
* Super Dooper Music Looper
* 2Simple Music Toolkit
* Musical Monsters

Stepping Stones and Goals

CD: recognise and explore how sounds can be changed; recognise repeated sounds and sound patterns and match movements to music; respond in a variety of ways to what they see, hear, smell, touch and feel.

CLL: listen with enjoyment, and respond to stories, songs and other music.

What you do

Wolfgang Amadeus Mozart was only five when he composed his first piece of music, the same age as some of the children in your group!

1. **Music Appreciation**
   o Use listening to music, and responding to it (through dance or other creative arts) as your starting point for the children's compositions. For example, play one of the animals' music from Carnival of the Animals and get the children to draw which animal they think the piece of music is. Or they could pretend to be, or dance to the different characters in Peter and the Wolf.

2. Based on the ideas in the music appreciation (e.g. animals, robots, seasons etc.) get the children to **make a composition** round that theme.
   o Use the response as an inspiration for the children. For example, let them see the animal they've drawn while they compose the music, or play the video of them acting or dancing. Ask them what it felt like.
   o Get the children to use the music software (any of the three above will work), to compose the piece of music. The music could be based around a book. For example, after listening and responding to Vivaldi's Four Seasons, try and get the children to compose a piece of music for each of the different kinds of weather in 'Mr Wolf's Week' (by Colin Hawkins).

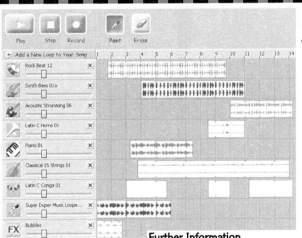

More ideas

* If you've based your composition on a book or a made up story, perform the story to parents, accompanied by the children's composition to make a musical show.

Further Information
Super Dooper Music Looper, available from Software Paradise, www.softwareparadise.co.uk (cost £34.95)

Music Toolkit available from 2Simple, www.2simple.com (cost £39)

Musical monsters, available from Q&D Multimead, www.q-and-d.co.uk (cost £35)

15. Technology walkabout

Help children to become aware of the different uses of ICT in everyday life

What you need

Technology is everywhere. Children are excited about technology, but they also take it for granted. What we think of as amazing, children treat as normal. We remember a time when some things weren't possible, because the technology had not been invented - being able to phone someone from anywhere on a mobile phone, using a microwave, taking a digital photo. Children don't know what life was like before. They need support to become aware of the technology around them, not just computers. We need to bring other sorts of ICT to their notice - everyday things such as microwaves, videos, photocopiers, telephones etc.

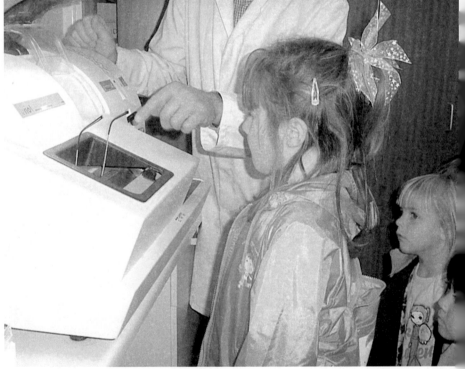

Stepping Stones and Goals

K&U: show an interest in ICT;
find out about and identify the uses of everyday technology.

What you do

1. **Start in your own setting:**
   - Your own setting will have masses of technology.
     Point out the different technologies to the children and talk about what it is for, and what life would it be like without it. Look at microwaves, telephones, word processors, security alarms and cameras, door locks, photocopiers, fax machines, CD players etc.
2. **Look at your own locality:**
   - If possible, arrange a walk around your own locality, and point out the different technologies available. Talk with them about why they're available, and what it would be like without them. Look at crossing signs, traffic lights, security cameras, parking barriers, meters, petrol pumps, street signs etc.
3. **Arrange a visit:**
   - All local businesses and public services use technology in some form or other. However, some might be more exciting than others! Try and arrange a visit to look at the different technology, how it's used, and how it helps the people who work there. Here are some ideas of visits that are tried and tested: supermarket, newspaper, nurseries (the plant kind) and fire station. Look at tills, automatic and revolving doors, pagers, intercoms, phones, scanners, scales, ticket printers etc.

More ideas

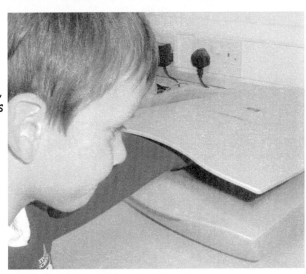

* Take photographs while you are with the children of the different technologies, and use the photographs to make a book, like in Activity 1. Or the children could use ICT to draw and write about what they have found out, as in Activity 6.

Further Information
Have a look at
www.hitchams.suffolk.sch.uk/control to find out how a plant nursery uses control technology to grow plants.

16. Make a pudding

Use everyday non-computer ICT tools to create something to eat

What you need
- microwave oven
- digital kitchen scales
- ingredients to make chocolate flapjacks:

- o 75g margarine
- o 2 tbsp of golden syrup
- o 75g of light brown sugar
- o 150g of porridge oats
- o 50g raisins
- o 100g chocolate (milk or plain)

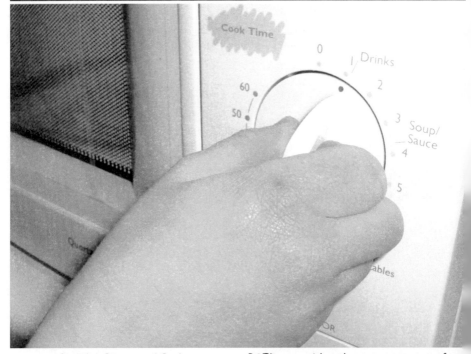

Stepping Stones and Goals

MD: recognise numerals 1-9;
order 2 items by weight or capacity.

K&U: use simple tools and techniques competently and appropriately
talk about what is seen & what is happening;
show an awareness of change.

PSED: consider the consequences of their words & actions for themselves & others;
show care and concern for self.

Additional Learning Intentions
Realise that many everyday items, such as a microwave, are examples of ICT and that they need to be programmed to work.

What you do

Health and Safety: In this activity the children will be heating food. You need extra adults, and you must follow the procedures in your setting for Health and Safety and for preparing food. Make sure that:
- all surfaces are thoroughly clean;
- hands are clean and long hair is tied back;
- children do not handle hot foods;
- any food allergies are known to <u>all</u> adults involved.

1. Do this activity in small groups. Some stages will have to be done by the adult helper as they involve hot ingredients. The adult can talk through these parts as the children stay at a safe distance. **Concentrate on the changes such as melting, combining, changing colour.**
2. **Help the children to weigh the butter, syrup and sugar** using the digital scales.
3. **Mix the butter, syrup and sugar** in a bowl.
4. **Cook the mixture** on high power in the microwave for 1-2 minutes, or until the mixture has melted.
5. **Stir in the oats and raisins** (an adult will need to do this as the mixture will be hot). Talk with the children about the differences they notice.
6. **Press into a 20cm, non-metallic, round dish.** The mixture will be cooler, so the children can do some of this stage.
7. **Cook on high power for 3-4 minutes, or until the centre is bubbling.** Remove from microwave.
8. **Break the chocolate** into a small bowl and **melt** in the microwave on high for about 30 seconds until melted.
9. **Pour the chocolate** over the top of the oat mixture.
10. Allow to **cool slightly** before cutting into pieces.
11. Health and safety doesn't allow children to lick spoons with hot melted chocolate on them, so you may have to do this bit for them!!

More ideas

* Cook food in a microwave to use for celebrations and festivals ; jelly for a party (add fruit for creativity and variety), or toffee apples for Bonfire Night.

Use an Internet search engine, such as Google, to look for recipes for different events; the Internet has a wealth of recipes for children.

Further Information
Google search engine
www.google.com

17. Understanding belief

Use ICT to find out more about other people's beliefs and cultures

> ### What you need
> - a local place of worship to visit
> - internet access

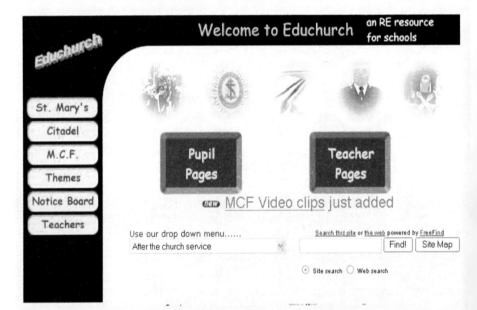

Stepping Stones and Goals

PSED: have a developing respect for their own cultures and beliefs and those of other people; have an awareness of, & show interest & enjoyment in cultural & religious differences; understand that people have different needs, views, cultures and beliefs, that need to be treated with respect.

K&U: gain an awareness of the cultures and beliefs of others.

Additional Learning Intentions

Start to understand that, although it is difficult to visit interesting places that aren't nearby, this can be done virtually using the Internet.

What you do

Make your real and virtual visits to new places short and active. Some young children find new experiences stressful and this may make them behave differently from normal! With young children it's always better to make several short visits than a long one which over-stretches their concentration and may make them resistant to further excursions.

1. **Before you go to visit a new place,** try to show the children pictures, video, or objects of what they might see. If some of the children are familiar with the place you plan to visit, let them tell the others about what happens there. If possible, take the chidlren to the place and look at the outside first.

2. **Now make a short, focused visit** to your chosen place of worship.

3. **Take photographs or video** while you're there so you can remind the children later of what you've seen and found out. (Ask first!)

4. **Interview someone from that place of worship** if you can, to find out more about it. Ask them about their faith, what's special to them and why, and about what they do in their place of worship.

5. Ask your visitor to **make the visit very visual,** bringing in the objects and symbols they would use.

6. **Go on a virtual tour of a contrasting place of worship.** Educhurch is a large Website written for schools, which compares and contrasts three very different Christian churches. You can interview the leader of the church virtually, and it also has video clips of different parts of the service. Alternatively you can visit a mosque or synagogue.

7. **Encourage the children to ask questions** about the contrasting places of worship. Use the sugestions in Activity 12, 'Developing Thinking Skills', to help you.

   Hint: if you haven't got fast Internet access in your setting to view the Educhurch video clips, why not ask a local school that has Broadband (many do now), or use a Broadband service at home, to download the video clips, write them onto a CD and use them in your setting.

8. Make a book or display about different places of worship. Look at Activity 1, 'Produce a class book' for some ideas on how to do this.

Further Information
Educhurch:
   www.educhurch.org.uk also has lots of video clips that can be played on the computer
Virtual mosque:
   www.hitchams.suffolk.sch.uk/mosque
Virtual synagogue:
   www.hitchams.suffolk.sch.uk/synagogue - has two different reading levels and a glossary of Jewish objects.
For more ideas on using ICT for RE in the Foundation Stage, look at:
   www.hitchams.suffolk.sch.uk/foundation/re

18. Be a movie director

Digital video and video editing are becoming cheaper all the time

Stepping Stones and Goals

CLL: have emerging self-confidence to speak to others about wants and interests;
enjoy listening to & using spoken language, and readily turn to it in their play;
speak clearly and audibly with confidence and control and show awareness of the listener;
use language to imagine and recreate roles and experiences.

Additional Learning Intentions

Start to use digital video as a creative medium.

What you do

Digital video: With the advent of the Digital Blue video camera, and its amazingly simple software for video editing, it is now possible for any age, any level of ICT confidence, and any budget to start creating their own digital movies. Who knows, one of your children might be the next Peter Jackson and create the next Lord of the Rings trilogy!

As well as digital video enhancing and developing speaking and listening skills and roleplay, it is also a valuable tool for assessment, presentation and feedback to parents, and a means of recording valuable learning experiences for later use.

Digital Blue is not the only cheap way of recording digital video. Many digital cameras now record video clips as well, and there is a plethora of cheap digital movie cameras on the market, like the Digital Blue. Microsoft has produced free, easy Movie editing software called Movie Maker 2 which can be downloaded and used to easily produce quality digital video clips.

1. Choose suitable activities for the children to video (almost anything that is clearly visible) - roleplay, an outing, practical maths work, music, a science experiment etc.

   a. Stress the importance of keeping the camera still when taking video shots; children have a habit of spinning the camera wildly around making the viewer feel quite ill!

   b. Remember that you can also take photographs with the video camera and use those in your final production too.

2. Support the children in downloading the video clips to the computer.

3. Show them how to view a video clip, and how to drag and drop it onto the timeline.

4. Help the children if they need to add effects or captions to the shots.

5. Show the final films to other children or parents.

More ideas

* Digital video is a great way of recording learning experiences which are not easily repeated. For example, visits to other places and visitors to your school. Many settings have one off events that may never be repeated again. Videoing these can be of real benefit as a resource for later, perhaps to remind your current children what happened, or to show to other children in years to come.

Further Information

Digital Blue video camera from Tag Learning, www.taglearning.com (price £84.95)

Additional help and advice for this activity on page 64

Movie Maker 2 can be downloaded for FREE from: www.microsoft.com/moviemaker. Remember, strange as it sounds, you don't even need a digital video camera to make your first film; still pictures will do, and, with a cheap microphone, you can get the children to record a narration.

For an example of how a video of a visitor can be used as a resource at a later date, look at these examples of a lady talking about living in Jamaica as a little girl: www.hitchams.suffolk.sch.uk/jamaica/video_clips.htm

19. Town planning

Use ICT to find out more about houses, homes and towns

Stepping Stones and Goals

K&U: observe, find out about and identify features in the place they live and the natural world; find out about their environment, and talk about those local features they like and dislike;

CD: understand that different media can be combined; make constructions, collages, paintings, drawings and dances.

Additional Learning Intentions

Use ICT to model town planning and house decoration.

What you do

1. Give a house a virtual make-over:
   a. Collect photographs of different types of local homes. Either walk around your local town taking photos, ask the children to bring in a photo of their house, or go to an estate agent and ask for photographs of properties for sale.
   b. Introduce the children to the artist Hundertwasser, and show how Hundertwasser tried to decorate houses by getting rid of the regular straight lines.
   c. Help the children to choose a house from a selection, and decorate it in the style of Hundertwasser, using a paint program, such as Revelation Natural Art,

2. Sort and label different houses using the two Publisher files:
   a. There are two versions of 'Sorting Homes'. They both have a set of different houses, which can be sorted into the two columns using different criteria. The second 'house sort' file allows you to label the two columns.
   b. Download from the Hitcham's homes website the file 'Labelling homes using Publisher'. This has four house pictures (two on the first file , and two on the second), and a set of labels, such as big, small, garage, porch, etc. These labels can be dragged to the appropriate house image. All labels have icons attached to them to help with reading.
   c. If you want to, you can delete the pictures that are contained in the different files, and put in your own houses. These activities don't need to be printed out (unless you want to!). They are designed to stimulate discussion between children and adults.

3. Decide where new buildings are going to be built in a town:
   a. Download the file New Buildings from the Hitcham's Felixstowe website. Get the children to examine the map closely, and then decide where they are going to put their new developments, e.g. supermarket, camp site or rubbish dump. They do this by dragging the appropriate icons to the correct place on the map.
   b. As before, these are primarily used to promote discussion, and can be changed to show your own local map.

4. Get the children to design their own towns. Although primarily a train game, Lego Loco has a great town deign section. You can use it to build houses, factories, path and road networks, public amenities such as the fire station and post office etc. You can also use trees, plants and fountains in your design. On closing down the Lego toolbox your invented town starts to become populated with people, animals and cars.

Further Information
Lego Loco available from REM;
   www.r-e-m.co.uk (cost £8.50)
Further information on Revelation Natural Art: www.hitchams.suffolk.sch.uk/ict_art/rna (£55)
Find out more about Lego Loco: www.hitchams.suffolk.sch.uk/foundation/lego_loco_help.htm
Downloads and further information about using ICT in Geography can be found at:
   www.hitchams.suffolk.sch.uk/ictgeography

20. Have an activity day

Be creative and do something you and the children are passionate about

What you need

anything goes! You choose a focus and select resources to fit.

Stepping Stones and Goals
For once, don't worry about them!
Additional Learning Intentions
It's fine to let go of the curriculum for a day and do something different. Do something that you and the children really fancy doing for a whole day!

What you do

1. Every once in a while it's great just to forget about national curriculum requirements, choose a theme, dress up with the children and do the things you always want to do, but never seem to have the time:
   - Do that really huge whole class painting indoors or outside.
   - You love cooking. Get involved in a day of simple recipes and end with a picnic.
   - Take the children to the local park or playground. Let them play and take photos or video.
   - You're passionate about your local rugby, football or tennis team. Take them to the sports club and get one of the players to teach the children some of the skills.
   - If you love music. Have a music day. Spend all day making up songs, composing music, getting all the instruments out. Play them your favourite music. Get them to draw a picture of what they see when they hear it.
   - Have a parade. Spend the morning making flags, banners, hats, masks and costumes. Then find some music and songs. Let the parade begin!
2. Try to include some ICT in your special day. Use a digital camera to take photographs of everyone enjoying it! Make a video, record the singing and dancing.
3. Have a look through this book and think of ways to adapt ideas it contains to fit in with your theme. If you're not sure how to do it, there'll probably be a parent out there who'll know how to help.

Further Information

The theme days (and weeks) at Hitchams School involve KS1 and KS2 children as well as Foundation children, the websites below will give you ideas for some of the things you can do.

* Art Day - www.hitchams.suffolk.sch.uk/schoolwork/art_day
* Asian week - www.hitchams.suffolk.sch.uk/asia
* Circus week - www.hitchams.suffolk.sch.uk/circus
* Fantasy Day - www.hitchams.suffolk.sch.uk/schoolwork/fantasy
* Nature week - www.hitchams.suffolk.sch.uk/envarea/natureweek
* Music Day - www.hitchams.suffolk.sch.uk/musicschoolwork/musicday
* Silver Day - www.hitchams.suffolk.sch.uk/silver

21. Keyboard creativity

Encourage the children to use a computer keyboard freely to explore reading and writing

Monday 9jmzprttty	Thursdaythursday drthuvswe
Tuesday 2dddy	Friday \\\zzzzzzxxxxxxcccccvvvvvbbbbbbbb bbbbbbbbbnnnnnnnnnnnnnnnnnnnnnmm mmmmm,,,,,,,,,............/////////////
Wednesday GEORGE4	Saturday	Sunday

Stepping Stones and Goals

CLL: attempt writing for different purposes, using features of different forms such as lists, stories and instructions; know that print carries meaning and, in English, is read from left to right and top to bottom.

Additional Learning Intentions

Build confidence with a computer keyboard and start to know where some letters are.

What you do

1. Encourage the children to write freely on a computer using the keyboard. Have a 'free access' writing area with plenty of writing materials including a computer and printer:
   o Try adapting the computer area into a writing area with paper, pens, pencils, typewriters, and of course the computer and printer.
   o Or experiment with making the computer area into a role-play area.
2. Don't forget to offer writing in all your role-play scenarios:
   o Computers are now in all environments: doctors, travel agents, libraries etc. Roleplay areas need to reflect this.
   o Try using templates, it's a great way to encourage children to have a try at the keyboard. For example, for a doctor's prescription, make a table in Word and save it with places to write the name, prescription and instructions for taking the medicine. Have a look at: www.hitchams.suffolk.sch.uk/foundation/literacy/reading_roleplay.htm and download some examples.
3. Keyboard Crazy is a great way for children to get to know the keyboard. It comes with lots of ideas on different ways to use it and lots of different cards to support the learning of lower case and upper case letters as well as a picture alphabet.
4. As well as using tables to encourage writing, try inserting pictures (ones they've taken or off the Internet) for writing captions.
5. Many early years writing programs have speech capabilities. These can often be changed in options to read each letter, word or sentence.
6. Lower case keyboards and large button keyboards can be a help, but a keyboard with upper case letters can be a teaching point.
7. 2Publish, part of the Infant Video toolkit from 2Simple, has great facilities for mixing text and images that the children have drawn. Clicking on the 'new page' button in the software brings up a menu with different templates such as: invitations, cartoon strips, speech bubbles, wanted posters, newspapers and much more!
8. Story Maker is a great program that allows children to build pictures using clipart and backgrounds, and then write stories and speech bubbles.
9. If you're lucky enough to have an interactive whiteboard or a Tablet PC, get the children to write on those. As they get better, they might like to have a go at the 'handwriting recognition tools' that Interactive Whiteboards and tablet PCs offer.

a
ACBDEFGHIJKLM
NOPQRSTUVWYX
DDDY
125
37
MMMY
BRYN
85

Additional help and advice for this activity on page 64

22. Letter sounds

Use a Pixie* to teach phonics!

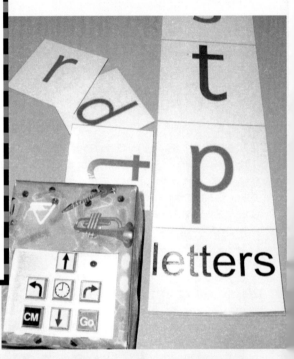

*Pixie: a PIXIE is a table-top size robot for the under-8s.

Stepping Stones and Goals

CLL: hear and say initial and final sounds in words, and short vowel sounds within words; link sounds to letters, naming and sounding the letters of the alphabet; use their phonic knowledge to write simple regular words & make phonetically plausible attempts at more complex words.

Additional Learning Intentions

Build confidence with a computer keyboard & start to know where some letters are.

What you do

1. **Play sound games** by recording different familiar sounds on to a tape, and then letting the children play the tape and try to recognise the sounds. Alternatively, get one group to make a sound tape for another group.
2. **Make a Pixie line and cards.** The Pixie line has on it letters of the alphabet, and the cards have the same letters. One child picks up a card and says the letter sound, and their partner has to move the Pixie to that letter by using the forward and back buttons. Each square on the Pixie line is the same length as the Pixie.
3. **2Publish has a template for making an alphabet book.** It allows the child to type in the letter, and draw pictures that start with that letter on the other side. To get the alphabet template, click on the new page button in Publisher. Once everyone has had a go, use the printouts to make an alphabet book.
4. There are many good **CDROMs** that help children to learn different letters and sounds. Try using Animated Alphabet from Sherston, or Magic Pencil from the BBC.

a b c d e f g h i j k l m n o p q r s t u v w x y z

alligator ★

An alligator is a large reptile, like a crocodile. Alligators and crocodiles live near rivers or swamps.

Surprise me   Back   Index   Home   Help   Options   Goodbye

More ideas

* Get a child to trace a letter in the sand and say the sound while you video them. Play back the videos in the class so other children can watch and trace the letters in the air with their finger.
* The Pixie line idea mentioned above can be used for lots of other areas of learning; finding out about numbers, counting on and back, colours - or how about minibeasts?

Further Information

2Publish, part of the Infant Video Toolkit available from www.2simple.com (cost £75)

Pixies available from
     www.swallow.co.uk (cost £136)

Download Pixies cards and lines (you'll need an A3 printer for the Pixie lines) from:
     www.hitchams.suffolk.sch.uk/foundation/pixie/pixie_downloads.htm

View a video clip of a Pixie line being used in a reception class:
     www.hitchams.suffolk.sch.uk/foundation/pixie

Animated Alphabet (£32) and Magic Pencil (£40) available from www.sherston.co.uk

The Little Book of ICT

23. Mixed up chameleon

Use a scanner to help children explore creative possibilities

What you need

- 🖱 art program eg Revelation Natural Art
- 🖱 scanner & printer
- 🖱 scissors & glue
- 🖱 an animal word bank to help with searches
- 🖱 images of animals in electronic form (eg using an image search on the Internet, or an electronic encyclopedia)

Stepping Stones and Goals

CD: explore colour, texture, shape, form and space in two or three dimensions.

CLL: listen with enjoyment, and respond to stories.

Additional Learning Intentions

Explore the idea that Art & ICT are not just something to be drawn and printed out, but that the print out can be manipulated and scanned back in.

What you do

1. Read the book, 'The Mixed up Chameleon' by Eric Carle.
2. Explain to the children that they are going to make up their own 'mixed up' animal.
3. Prepare a wordbank of animals with the children. Use pictures to help children recognise the words. You could use a 'pack of cards' style with the name of the animal and its picture on each card.
4. Encourage or help the children to choose a card of one of the animals and use the card to help them search, using a computer, for a digital photograph that the children could print out. The children might need to do this a few times so that they end up with a range of animals. Some children will need help!
5. Take a range of animal printouts, and cut out parts from each of them. The children might end up with the body of an elephant, legs from a horse, and the head of a giraffe.
6. Glue these body parts together to make a 'mixed up' animal. The children could use parts of the printouts of animals other children don't need.
7. Scan the mixed up animal back into the computer.
8. Open the scanned 'mixed up animal' into a paint program, such as Revelation Natural Art, and help them paint a background for their mixed up animal.

More ideas

* Use the 'Print out, do something to it, and scan it back in again' idea for other things. It is a great way to encourage children to be more creative with their printouts. For more ideas, look at the 'World of Pattern' websites below where all the ideas work well on printouts.
* Ask a parent or grandparent to read 'The Mixed up Chameleon' and record it onto tape so children can listen along with the book in the listening area (remember, the children hear you all day long!).

Further Information

World of Pattern Art & ICT Website which explores creative things to do with printouts and scanning in images which are then developed further in an art package, can be found at: www.hitchams.suffolk.sch.uk/ict_art/ideas/world_of_pattern.htm

More ideas on animal prints: www.hitchams.suffolk.sch.uk/ict_art/wingfield/ict_printouts.htm

Revelation Natural Art, available from: www.logotron.co.uk (cost £55)

Image searches available on the Internet: www.google.com or www.altavista.com

More examples of mixed up chameleons: www.hitchams.suffolk.sch.uk/ict_art/chameleon

24. Minibeasts

Look at everyday animals in and around your setting

<table>
<tr>
<td>

What you need
🖱 digital camera
🖱 digital microscope (optional)
🖱 'Bug boxes' for observation

</td>
<td>

🖱 My World 3, and My World science CDROM
🖱 2simple Infant Video Toolkit

</td>
</tr>
</table>

Stepping Stones and Goals

K&U: observe, find out about and identify features in the place they live and the natural world; find out about, and identify some features of living things, objects & events they observe.

MD: use language such as 'more' or 'less' to compare two numbers; count reliably up to 10 everyday objects.

Additional Learning Intentions
Use ICT for modelling and data handling activities.

What you do

1. **Talk with the children** about the sorts of animals they might see in and around your setting (don't foget the small creatures). Talk about how you could find out more about these animals.

2. **Go on some 'Bug Hunts'** and observe minibeasts from your local habitat. There are a number of things that the children could do:

   o Collect minibeasts in the observation 'bug boxes'. Examine, discuss and draw what they noticed.

   > Talk to the children about collecting minibeasts, never to touch them, & always put them back in the place they find them. Make sure the children can identify sting-ing insects, such as bees and wasps, and that they don't try and collect these!

   o Use a digital camera in 'macro' mode to get some good close up photos of the minibeasts. These can be used for display, identification and observation later. See activity 5 to find out more about macro mode.

   o Minibeasts can be seen really well using a cheap digital microscope. Use the digital microscope in conjunction with an Interactive Whiteboard. For the first time, you can talk about and observe minibeasts with a large group of children, and everyone can see!

   o Use 2Count to make a pictogram of how many minibeasts you have seen. There is no set minibeasts count, but it's easy to make one of your own by clicking the new sheet button, and selecting My Pictures. Remember, you can use photographs you've taken (using the 'open' button). Save your graph for later use.

3. Use the My World 3 Science CDROM to **explore a virtual habitat** (a file called More Minibeasts part 2). This way they can find things and explore areas that they perhaps wouldn't normally be able to.

4. Use 2Publish from the Infant Video Toolkit or **create a PowerPoint presentation** to write about the minibeasts they have found. Photographs that you have taken can be imported into 2Publish by selecting the right click option in the teachers options screen.

More ideas

* Support the children to take a photo-graph of a habitat, open it into a paint program that has clipart (Revelation Natural Art does), and putting clipart of minibeasts into appropriate loca-tions on the photograph.

Further Information

Infant Video Toolkit, available from:
www.2simple.com (cost £75)

QX5 computer microscope from Tag Learning:
www.taglearning.co.uk (cost: £80)

My World 3 and My World Science CDROM available from Granada Learning:
www.granada-learning.com (cost £49 and £39 respectively)

25. Let's go shopping

Use ICT to support role-play with number and money

What you need
🖱 electronic roleplay toys suitable for shopping such as electronic cash register, phone, answer machine, calculators (both sorts: big and chunky and one that prints out)

🖱 2Simple software
🖱 Percy's Money Box
🖱 My World 3
🖱 remote control cars, eg Lego buggies or Pixies
🖱 At the Café roleplay software

Stepping Stones and Goals

MD: say and use number names in order in familiar contexts;
count reliably up to 10 everyday objects;
recognise numerals 1 to 9;
use mathematical ideas & methods to solve practical problems;
in practical activities & discussions begin to use the vocabulary involved in adding & subtracting;
use language such as 'more' or 'less' to compare two numbers;
use language such as 'heavier' or 'lighter' to compare quantities.

What you do

1. Set up a shopping role-play area. This could contain:
   - An electronic cash register, for free and structured play with money, scanning, prices, totalling, change etc;
   - Calculators to find the totals;
   - 2Publish from the 2Simple Infant video toolkit, for making signs, labels and posters;
   - 2Count from the same software, for making graphs of stock levels;
   - Telephones to take/place orders;
   - Forms created using the tables tool in Word. Use these for reporting faulty/replaced items, appointment diaries, writing receipts etc.
2. Use the 'At the Café' roleplay software to support play in a café.
3. Use the My World 3 fruit sorting screen to sort fruit into different boxes. There are more fruits than boxes, and there are cakes that shouldn't be there at all! This encourages the children to choose different criteria for sorting fruit, such as colour, shape, size.
4. Use Percy's Moneybox to aid coin recognition and buying things.
5. Use the Remote control buggies, or a Pixie, as a shopping robot. Set up a 'microworld' for it to explore, visit shops and buy the things it needs. Once this has been done using robots, it can then be simulated using an on screen robot (using the 2Go software package).

More ideas

* Use 2Count for research to see which is the most popular type of food, so that they stock more of it in their shop. They could be finding out which are the most popular milks, and which are the favourite flavours to add to milk. Download prepared 2count pictograms for use with your 2simple software for this activity.

Further Information

Find electronic cash registers, and other electronic roleplay toys at the Early Learning Centre

2Count, 2Publish and 2Go are part of the Infant Video Toolkit from www.2simple.com (cost £75)

2Count downloads: www.hitchams.suffolk.sch.uk/foundation/2simple/2count.htm

Percy's Money Box available from Neptune computers: www.neptunect.co.uk (£29)

My World 3 and At the Café roleplay software from Granada Learning:
   www.granada-learning.com (cost £49 and £39)

Three Remote Controlled Buggies and Tech machine Sets from Commotion:
   www.commotiongroup.co.uk (cost £99.95)

Pixies available from: www.swallow.co.uk (cost £130)

26. Ourselves

Use ICT to support children's investigation of themselves

What you need

- My World 3
- Face Paint 2
- 2Count and 2Publish from the Infant video toolkit
- art Software
- digital Camera
- laminator
- digital stopwatch

Kiera feels ok.

Stepping Stones and Goals

PSED: have a developing awareness of their own needs, views & feelings & be sensitive to the needs, views & feelings of others.

CLL: read a range of familiar & common words & simple sentences.

CD: understand that different media can be combined.

PD: move with confidence & safety; move with control & co-ordination

What you do

1. My World 3 has two screens devoted to the body and the face. At its simplest level, a child can click on a body part, and the computer will tell them what it is. For older children, there is a labelling option with text and arrow cards.

2. Face Paint 2 is a program that allows children to explore a huge variety of faces and facial expressions. Children can select the type and colour of mouth, eyes, hair, and much more.

3. Examine how children's feelings change by making a feelings book. Take a photograph of everyone in the class and ask them how they are feeling. Make this into a book, which could be electronic using PowerPoint, or a paper based one using Word. Each page could be a picture of someone in the class, with a sentence underneath saying, e.g. Aaron feels angry. Look at the book the following week, and talk about whether the children are feeling the same or different.

4. Which eye colour do most children have? Which eye colour do fewest children have? Get the children to look into each others eyes and tell each other what colour eyes they have. Organise the children into human pictograms (get them lined up according to eye colour, and see which line is the longest/shortest). Then use the 2count eye colour pictogram, and get each child to come and click the colour of their eyes.

5. Provide opportunities for children to make a laminated dinner mat of themselves. Start with a brightly coloured sheet of paper, and onto it glue a photocopy of their hands, a picture they've drawn on the computer, a photograph a friend has taken of them, and their name, which they've written. Other photos of family, friends, pets, pop stars or favourite toys can also be included.

6. Program a digital stopwatch to count down from one minute. See how many times a child can write their name, skip, climb through a hoop; how many marbles they can pick up with a spoon and put in a container, etc. Use the 2publish page which is divided into four sections, and encourage the children to draw a picture of what they did, and write the number of times they did it.

Further Information

2Count and 2Publish are part of the Infant Video Toolkit from www.2simple.com (£75)
2Count downloads: www.hitchams.suffolk.sch.uk/foundation/2simple/2count.htm
My World 3 & Face Paint 2 from Granada Learning: www.granada-learning.com (£49 and £39)
More examples of place mats at: www.hitchams.suffolk.sch.uk/ict_art/placemats
Ideas on the 'Feelings book': www.hitchams.suffolk.sch.uk/foundation/re/feelings_book.htm

The Little Book of ICT

Essential Stuff!

Below you can find some key ICT equipment for a Foundation setting. The list is in no particular order, and assumes that you already have access to a computer. There is information on where to buy equipment, a rough guide to cost, and the activities in the book which use them. The list is a mixture of software, and hardware. Remember......It's not just computers!

Item	Brief description	Suppliers	Approx. cost	Activities
Tape recorder	It's a great idea to have a mixture of chunky early years tape recorders and small, handheld Dictaphones.	Early Learning Centre	£20	3, 5 and 23
Digital camera	Allows you to take photos and instantly download them to a computer for viewing/ printing. Some don't even need a computer, and print straight to the printer. Cheap ones are fine, more expensive ones might allow you to record digital video as well.	Computer shop, camera shop or Mail order	£100 +	1, 2, 3, 5, 6, 10, 13, 15, 18 (digital video) 23, 24 and 26
Pixie	A programmable robot that's very easy to use, and has many more applications than just making it move!	www.swallow.co.uk	£136	8, 9, 10, and 22
Infant video toolkit	A suite of software programs for Early Years. It's a bit like Microsoft Office, a set of essential tools, but for young children. It includes painting, publishing (painting and writing), graphing, and simple control.	www.2simple.com	£75	2, 6, 9, 10, 11, 13, 15, 19, 22, 24, 25 and 26
My World 3	A drag and drop program that allows you to manipulate objects on a screen. The basic My World comes with lots of screen already set up, but you can also buy lots of extras quite cheaply.	www.granada-learning.com	My World 3, £49 £39 for add-ons	9, 11, 24, 25 and 26
Electronic role-play toys	A great way of enhancing roleplay and bring it into the 21st century. A variety of electronic role-play equipment is available, from electronic cash register, to an answer phone, to a microwave.	Early Learning Centre	Various between £7 and £15	3
CDROM books	A great way for children to interact with a book. Recommendations would include Grandma & Me for fiction, and My First Dictionary for non-fiction.	www.r-e-m.co.uk	Grandma & me- £12 My First Dictionary - £20	6, 12 and 22

Here is a list of other ICT items that are great to have in a Foundation setting, although not as essential to get started. Again, it's in no particular order.

Item	Brief description	Suppliers	Approx. cost	Activities
Interactive Whiteboard	This is a very valuable piece of technology in the foundation setting, and is used very differently when compared to other Key Stages. Social interaction, doing things such as ICT painting on a very large scale, the way a child interacts with the technology are just some of the plusses. It only didn't make the first list because of the price!	There are many suppliers, but for a start, try Matrix, who have a wide range. www.matrixdisplay.com	£1500+	All!
Clicker 5	An essential writing tool to support children when they're ready to start writing. A writing program that has word banks on screen, and speech to support the early development of writing. It can also be used to make electronic books.	www.cricksoft.com	£120	5 and 9
Musical Keyboard	Get a good music keyboard and children will be able to explore music in a variety of ways, from creating their own melodies and rhythms, to singing along to well known tunes.	There are lots of child friendly keyboards. Have a look at the Early Learning Centre one.	£20	4
Remote Control Car	Used well, it can be great for lots of things: fine motor skills, maths, exploring imaginary worlds to name but a few. Make sure the one you buy is sturdy enough to last!	Again there are lots, but you can't beat the Lego Duplo Remote Controlled Buggy and the Tech Machines set from Commotion for durability. We've had ours for years, and they're still going strong. www.commotiongroup.co.uk	£100	8, 10, 11 and 25

This list is in no way definitive, and there are many more items that could be added: some phonics and numeracy software, the 'At The....(Café, Vets, Doctors) roleplay software series, Revelation Natural Art (wonderfully natural, and easy to use drawing software), cheap digital video cameras and digital microscope, outdoor ICT hardware (metal detectors and walkie-talkies)....... The list could go on and on!

How can you afford it all? Like all things, start slowly, bit by bit. However, remember that ICT lending libraries for Foundation settings are becoming more and more common. Look out for one in your area, and make good use of it.

Activity 1 (page 8/9) - A Book About:... : Further Information
Support on using **Word**:
> www.hitchams.suffolk.sch.uk/helps/word

Support on using **PowerPoint**:
> www.hitchams.suffolk.sch.uk/helps/powerpoint

Support on using **Clicker 5:**
> www.hitchams.suffolk.sch.uk/helps/clickerere

Where to buy **microphones** for computers:
> Paul Godfrey, Suffolk Audio Visual, Tel:01502-405472

Kiera feels ok.

Activity 2 (page 10/11) - Be a Clown: Further Information
On **clown painting:**
> www.hitchams.suffolk.sch.uk/ict_art/clowns

On decorating **Indian Elephants**:
> www.hitchams.suffolk.sch.uk/ict_art/elephants

On **mendhi hands**:
> www.hitchams.suffolk.sch.uk/ict_art/mendhi

On **Revelation Natural Art**::
> www.hitchams.suffolk.sch.uk/ict_art/rna

More about **graphics Tablets**:
> www.hitchams.suffolk.sch.uk/ict_art/graphics_tablets.htm

Revelation Natural Art available from
> www.logotron.co.uk (cost £55)

More **Art & ICT ideas** for the foundation stage:
> www.hitchams.suffolk.sch.uk/ict_art/ideas/foundation.htm

Activity 9 (page 24/25) - Shape and Space:... :Further Information
My World 3 can be purchased from Granada Learning:
> www.granada-learning.com (cost £49)

Clicker 5 can be purchased from Cricksoft:
> www.cricksoft.com

Clicker Grids for Learning can be downloaded from:
> www.learninggrids.com
> although its much easier, quicker, and probably cheaper in the long run, to buy the Clicker Grids for Learning CDs from Cricksoft.

Revelation Natural Art can be purchased from Logotron:
> www.logotron.co.uk

2Paint and 2Go are part of the **2Simple** Infant video Toolkit. If you already have this program, make sure you have the latest version which has a lot more features and is Interactive Whitebaord friendly (it has a pull down chain which allows the children to pull down the screen to reach the top, and a pop-up keyboard).

2Go support Website for ideas, children's examples, and downloadable workcard:
> www.hitchams.suffolk.sch.uk/foundation/pixie/2simple/2go.htm

Pixie Centre for example video clips of ideas, and downloadable resources:
> www.hitchams.suffolk.sch.uk/foundation/pixie

Pixies can be bought from Swallow Systems:
> www.swallow.co.uk (cost £160)

Additional information for activities on pages 26/28/32

Activity 10 (page 26/27) - Our World: Further Information
Infant Video Toolkit , available from
>www.2simple.com (cost £75)

Three **Remote Controlled Buggies and Tech Machine Sets** can be purchased from Commotion:
>www.commotiongroup.co.uk (cost £99.95)

Pixies can be bought from Swallow Systems:
>www.swallow.co.uk (cost £160)

Here are 3 websites of **similar projects**, by older children (Year3/4), to give you some ideas:
Animal Roadkills:
>www.hitchams.suffolk.sch.uk/roadkill

Rural Public transport:
>www.hitchams.suffolk.sch.uk/transport/at

Crime Prevention:
>www.hitchams.suffolk.sch.uk/crime

Activity 11 (page 28/29) - Space Exploration: Further Information
>www.Nasa Kids: http://kids.mscf/nasa.gov/

Storymaker: Available from Spa Software,
>www.spasoft.co.uk (cost £39)

My World 3 can be purchased from Granada Learning:
>www.granada-learning.com

Infant Video Toolkit, available from
>www.2simple.com (cost £49)

Example of using **StoryMaker** with own photographs:
>www.hitchams.suffolk.sch.uk/ictgeography/felixstowe/felixstowe_stories.htm

Activity 13 (page 32/33) - Colour Matching: Further Information
Revelation Natural Art can be purchased from Logotron:
>www.logotron.co.uk (cost £55)

2Count, part of the Infant Video Toolkit available from
>www.2simple.com

Clicker 5 can be purchased from Cricksoft:
>www.cricksoft.com

Clicker Grids for Learning can be downloaded from:
>www.learninggrids.com
>Although its much easier, quicker, and probably cheaper in the long run, to buy the Clicker Grids for Learning CDs from Cricksoft.

More Art & ICT ideas for the foundation stage:
>www.hitchams.suffolk.sch.uk/ict_art/ideas/foundation.htm

The Primary Strategy CD - Learning and Teaching Using ICT; Example materials from Foundation Stage to Year 6. available: Tel:0845 60 222 60 or dfes@prolog.uk.com has some more ideas (including clips and examples from Hitchams)

Note: all addresses, sites and prices are correct at the time of printing
prices and availability may change

Additional information for activities on pages 42/48

Activity18 (page 42/43) - Be Movie Director: Further Information

Digital Blue video camera from Tag Learning:
www.taglearning.com, price (£84.95)

Movie Maker 2 can be downloaded for FREE from:
www.microsoft.com/moviemaker
Remember, strange as it sounds, you don't even need a digital video camera to make your first film; still pictures will do, and, with a cheap microphone, you can get the children to record a narration.
For an example of how a video of a visitor can be used as an educational resource at a later date, have a look at these examples of a lady talking about living in Jamaica as a girl:
www.hitchams.suffolk.sch.uk/jamaica/video_clips.htm

Activity 21 (page 48/49) - Keyboard Creativity: Further Information

2Publish, part of the Infant Video Toolkit ☐ available from:
www.2simple.com (cost £75)

Storymaker: Available from Spa Software:
www.spasoft.co.uk (cost £39)

Keyboard Crazy available from Keywise Systems:
www.keyboardcrazy.co.uk (cost for basic game £48)

Example of using a **Tablet PC** to write with:
www.hitchams.suffolk.sch.uk/foundation/wireless_technology.htm

**Note: all addresses, sites and prices are correct at the time of printing
prices and availability may change**

About the Author and the School

Andrew Trythall has been ICT co-ordinator at Sir Robert Hitcham's CEVAP School in Suffolk for eight years. During this time he has led both staff and pupils of the school in developing a very high standard of ICT throughout all subjects, as well as using technology to support a more open-ended, creative curriculum. Much of this work is reflected in the huge school website, to which all staff and pupils contribute. The website has over 3,000 pages, and recieves well over 6,000 hits a day.

As well as showing the work that goes on in the school, the web site has educational resources for pupils (e.g. 'Educhurch' and 'Skulls and Skeletons'), resources for teachers (e.g. using ICT in the Foundation Stage, Music and Art), as well as simple on-line support for using a range of educational software such as Paint Shop Pro and Microsoft Publisher.

For the last five years, Andrew has worked with a team of Foundation Stage practitioners and advisory staff from the local area to create, develop and test out ideas for using ICT in the Foundation Stage curriculum.

This book is a result of development work over the past five years.

The web site can be found at:www.hitchams.suffolk.sch.uk

If you have found this book useful you might also like ...

**The Little Book of
Science Through Art**
LB1
ISBN 1-902233-61-1

**The Little Book of
Investigations**
LB20
ISBN 1-904187-66-8

**The Little Book of
Time & Place**
LB31
ISBN 1-904187-95-1

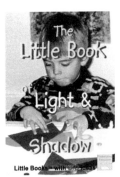

**The Little Book of
Light & Shadow**
LB25
ISBN 1-904187-81-1

All available from

Featherstone Education   PO Box 6350
Lutterworth LE17 6ZA
T:0185 888 1212   F:0185 888 1360

on our web site

www.featherstone.uk.com

and from selected
book suppliers

The Little Books Club

Little Books meet the need for exciting and practical activities which are fun to do, address the Early Learning Goals and can be followed in most settings. As one user put it

"When everything else falls apart I know I can reach for a Little Book and things will be fine!"

We publish 10 Little Books a year – one a month except for August and December. **Little Books Club members receive each <u>new</u> Little Book on approval at a reduced price** as soon as it is published.

Examine the book at your leisure. Keep it or return it. You decide.

That's all. No strings. No joining fee. No agreement to buy a set number of books during the year. And you can leave at any time.

Little Books Club members receive -

- ♥ *each new Little Book on approval as soon as it's published*
- ♥ *a specially reduced price on that book and on any other Little Books they buy*
- ♥ *a regular, free newsletter dealing with club news and aspects of Early Years curriculum and practice*
- ♥ *free postage on anything ordered from our catalogue*
- ♥ *a discount voucher on joining which can be used to buy from our catalogue*
- ♥ *at least one other special offer every month*

There's always something in Little Books to help and inspire you!

Phone 0185 888 1212 for details